"A Wall in Naples," c. 1782 by   Thomas Jones (1742-1803)
By kind permission of   The National Gallery, London
                                        Photo©The National Gallery

Author photo by   Alan Halsey

Published in the United States by   Fence Books
                                        303 East Eighth Street, #B1
                                        New York, NY 10009
                                        www.fencebooks.com

Book design by   Rebecca Wolff

Fence Books are distributed by   University Press of New England
                                        www.upne.com

and printed in Canada by   Westcan Printing Group
                                        www.westcanpg.com

Library of Congress Cataloguing in Publication Data
      Corless-Smith, Martin [1965–]
      Swallows / Martin Corless-Smith

Library of Congress Control Number: 2005933980

ISBN 0-9771064-2-X

FIRST EDITION

Earlier versions of some of these poems appeared in *GutCult.com* and *Kiosk*. Thanks to the editors of these journals, and to Catherine Wagner, Joshua Beckman, and Rebecca Wolff, who helped me put this book together. And thanks to Romayne Licudi, in whose house much of this writing took place.

SWALLOWS

MARTIN CORLESS-SMITH

for Ambrose

SWALLOWS

we are swallowed up irreparably, irrevocably, irremediably . . . envy the sparrows and the swallows, yea.

—John Donne, *Sermon LXVI (1626)*

The sparrow hath found a house and the swallow a nest for herself
—*Psalm 84*

Gellius is of the opinion that Toxius, son of Uranus, was the inventor of building with clay, having taken as his example the construction of swallows' nests.

—Pliny the Elder, *The Natural History*

Though useless to us, and rather of molestation, we commonly refrain from killing Swallows, and esteem it unlucky to destroy them: whether herein there be not a Pagan relique, we have some reason to doubt. For we read in Elian, that these birds were sacred unto the *Penates* or household gods of the ancients, and therefore were preserved. The same they also honoured as the nuncio's of the spring; and we find in Athenæus that the Rhodians had a solemn song to welcome in the Swallow.

—Sir Thomas Browne, *Pseudodoxia Epidemica*

Conrad Gesner mentions that the swallow remains in her nest all winter as though dead, and revives in the spring; this is to be accounted a great marvel, 'ac imaginem resurrectionis nostrorum corporum'. (*Historiæ Animalium* Lib. III. qui est de Auium natura, 1585, pp.549-50)

Birds that sing as they fly are few: Swallow *Hirundo domestica:* In soft
sunny weather . . .

Dear Sir,

The house-swallow, or chimney swallow is undoubtedly the first comer of all British hirundines . . . It is worth remarking that these birds are seen first about lakes and mill-ponds . . . though called the chimney swallow, [she] by no means builds altogether in chimnies, but often within barns and out-houses against the rafters; and so she did in Virgil's time; . . . Ante/ Garrula quam tignis nidos suspendat hirundo. [Before the twittering swallow hangs its nest from the rafters *Georgics* 4] . . . As to the quote it is difficult to say precisely which species *hirundo* Virgil might intend . . . the ancients did not attend to specific differences like modern naturalists: yet somewhat may be gathered, enough to incline me to suppose that . . . the poet had his eye on the swallow. In the first place the epithet *garrula* suits the swallow well who is a great songster; and not the martin, which is a rather mute bird; and when it sings is so inward as scarce to be heard.

—Gilbert White, *The Natural History of Selbourne*

Chateaubriand in *Itinéraire de Paris à Jérusalem* reports how, in crossing the Peloponnesus in search of Greece's glorious past, he was struck by the sight of a huge crowd of birds covering the river Pamisus. Despite our best attempts, the description falls short. Chateaubriand is touched not so much by the multiplicity of species and the variety of plumages as by the very idea of migration: "One such American bird may have attracted Aristotle's attention on a Greek river bank when the philosopher did not even suspect the existence of a New World."

Thus birds knew before mankind the true expanse of man's home. This motif reveals human weakness in the most learned and wise of men. Chateaubriand, by seeing in migrating birds the guardians of the unity of the world, enriches a theme which, in western literature's repertory of topoi, incarnates the cyclical time distinguishing the natural world from the human world. Michelet, in his beautiful ode to the returning swallow, recounts how "these faithful birds, of persevering memory," returning generation after generation to build their nests under the same eaves—while the house during the same period changes owners several times—become the symbol of the home's stability, even though they are nomads.

—Christophe Pradeau, *Judith Schalanger: Explorer of Lettered Space*

Theirs is the hearth. Where the mother has built her nest, the daughter and the granddaughter build. They return there every year; their generations succeed to it more regularly than do our own. A family dies out or is dispersed, the mansion passes into other hands; but the swallow constantly returns to it, and maintains its right of occupation.

It is thus that the traveler has come to be accepted as a symbol of the permanency of home. She clings to it with such fidelity, that though the home may be repaired, or partially demolished, or long disturbed by masons, it is still retaken possession, or re-occupied by these faithful birds of persevering memory.

She is the bird of return. And if I bestow this title upon her, it is not alone on account of her annual return, but on account of her general conduct, and the direction of her flight, so varied, yet nevertheless circular, and always returning upon itself . . . this revolving flight, this incessantly returning movement has always attracted our eyes and heart, throwing us into reverie, into a world of thought . . . Is it a bird? Is it a spirit? Ah, if thou art a soul . . .

—Jules Michelet, *The Swallow*

Sept. 3.—Cloudy and wet, and wind due east; air without palpable fog, but very heavy with moisture—welcome for a change. Forenoon, crossing the Delaware, I noticed unusual numbers of swallows in flight, circling, darting, graceful beyond description, close to the water. Thick around the bows of the ferry-boat as she lay tied in her slip, they flew; and as we went out I watch'd beyond the pier-heads, and across the broad stream, their swift-winding loop-ribands of motion, down close to it, cutting and intersecting. Though I had seen swallows all my life, seem'd as though I never before realized their peculiar beauty and character in the landscape. (Some time ago, for an hour, in a huge old country barn, watching these birds flying recall'd the 22d book of the Odyssey, where Ulysses slays the suitors, bringing things to *claircissement,* and Minerva, swallow-bodied, darts through the spaces of the hall, sits high on a beam, looks complacently on the show of slaughter, and feels in her element, exulting, joyous.)

—Walt Whitman, *Specimen Days*

At earlier times, in the summer evenings during my childhood when I had watched from the valley as swallows circled in the last light, still in great numbers in those days, I would imagine that the world was held together by the courses they flew through the air.

—W. G. Sebald, *The Rings of Saturn*

Nothing is esteemed in this lunatic age but what is kept in
Cabinets
—Michael Drayton, *Poly-Olbion*

KUNSTKAMMER

Ah, land of whirring wings
beyond the rivers of Ethiopia,
sending ambassadors by the Nile
in vessels of papyrus on the waters!
Go, you swift messengers.

Isaiah 18.1-2

FROM PAPYRI

the (thoughtless & Immortal) Cockerels shout (& shouting)
this morning (dawn allover Kalamaki Town)—Ranting
drunks or lone catastrophes

~

Who is it here below the ground, who spoke with a voice divine
to amaze us?

(animal call, cow—it is evening, though still immensely hot)

~

A cockerel with a dog's head passed out from the shade
of "2 brothers Inn" A dream of a city of Cockerels—

a sand coloured spider visible by the shadow it casts on the dirt
An idle spirit persuades you to bear it lightly

My quarrels I dissolve, and my former deeds.

~

There (the Goat again)

(Island of Cats, Rats, I contemplate action)

~

(My greatest delight now is to listen to the intimacy of others—ear
against the wall—breath held) But there are no secrets divulged

Archemorus[1] shall be his name hereafter (The name is derived from
archein—begin and moros—doom)

The sky was torn asunder by northern gales—I see a figure
hastening hither apace—It were a shame for me to return home
with excuses on my lips.

~

Now I would go forth into the fields to listen to my own foolish heart
Far from home my life was settled. Yet I turned and return as I must

These things are done in secret: whom do you fear?

~

my mind beat against the sea wall—what is this—
how far to drop—the next and the next.

Our daughter passed me in the street
awkward with her handbag—child still
with her shoulders high—(o) dear stranger

"You have brought an army to attack your own country"

~

God devoured his son alive
and you cried your approval. . . This is our first excuse

~

———————————————

[1] Pseudo-Epiphanius

Well, here is solitude; whatever I say, there's nobody here to listen.
There seems no difference between the beautiful, the good, the holy and the
evil I have been dead the whole of my life so far invisible.

(As I spring into life momentarily as an aphid)

I never discovered the sun before—so big, so fine!

(None of man's miseries is past belief)

~

He thought that he was smiting serpents; but they were his children. . . .

~

Where the fields   Which decay   Not, nor fade
receive in their embrace . . . I arrive on scene after scene
of near perfection—eagerly—The Train—
Far . . . of many trees . . . caught by night beside these
vessels unforgettable.

~

There grew a corn-ear with barley, all seeds together, there
flowers the white-coated wheat together with the dark-haired
barley . . . nature *is* precise.

~

hostile swarm of cranes that devour the wheat . . . awoke, so great a song
a hymn (singing a hymn) of harvest . . .

~

birds nimble and musical . . . perched on the topmost pine . . .
in loud sweet jargoning . . . hidden in the darkness of the Book.
. . . Along the oblique pathway . . . was amazed, on the right side by
a swallow . . . who skim deep waters . . . of many hues and many
guises . . . of all things the beginning and the end are yours.

A SELECTION OF THE APHORISMS OF PSEUDO-EPIPHANIUS

We become subject, more than we are aware, to idols of the theatre.

(A) room is a doorway.

The mind is written (read) on the body.

Our (real) house has no walls.

We are (the same) as grass. We are very much as cattle.

Efforts of understanding (are) born out of futility where they remain.

The spirit dwells in activity (of the body/the world).

Your meaning, when you speak, is that you speak.

Without is contained all that is within.

Our features are war, famine, hatred, sadness as well as play, harvest, love and pleasure.

Happiness accepts strife.

(In) change (something) always persists.

Lightning . . . a career . . . (an island)

The web is no mistake between the leaves.

Of another colour, of another temperature is else.

Peace is a quiet war.

If we must see the universe as a human, let it be an imbecile.

Qualities are not apart from our understanding (are not away from our noticing).

Our idea of the human is the human. Our idea of the cow is such.

An event may be seen as fortuitous or accidental.

Things are in harmony without the pleasure of (our) agreement.

Knowledge is a sensation of ignorance.

All Things (something) are in the process of change, our understanding of which is to observe them (it) between two imagined poles.

Because we remember we believe we endure. Memory is a comparison of moments, not a store of ages.

The only necessity is that which is next.

If Man is moral fire is moral.

Can we then separate Water, Earth, Fire and Air? Only in their instant. And then onward. One is always in brittle contact with its most elusive other aspect.

Is our seeing anything less than the energy to see?

There is no difference between self-knowledge and knowledge of the world. Can you see behind your eyes?

Desire is coterminous with movement. Satisfaction is other than desire.

Is my living discernible from yours?

Soul is that name which I give to all that beneath all I am . . .

Myself is an accidental outcome though my responsibilities are true.

If I am wholly free I am only partially aware of this.

If you don't compromise might you live forever?

Man is frail and the law of the universe is mutability.

The things you have decided are not necessary.

The clocks described by Ktesibios and Hero
had no scale of hours to show
no means of indicating time
so much as to possess it or embody it somehow

Possibly the world has neither beginning nor end (Xenophanes)
Or it was given birth by Chaos (Hesiod)
Or it is composed of atoms (Leucippus)
Or it is composed of fire (Heraclitus)
Or it is composed of water (Thales)
Or it is composed of four elements (Empedocles)

Melancholy was an angle fixed upon the point of her own contemplation
Nicholas of Cusa praised docta ignorantia
Montaigne provided a learned proof of universal ignorance and uncertainty
Cornelius Agrippa proved the inadequacies of all learning
Erasmus praised at once folly and by indirection wisdom beyond all men
Sebastian Brandt saw the world a ship full of fools
insist upon it

Of Biblical Prophecy:

It was the job of mathematicians and chronologers, like Napier, Brightman, Mede, Ussher and Newton. Such men believed in the possibility of establishing a science of prophecy, just as Hobbes believed in the possibility of establishing a science of politics. Both hopes proved unrealizeable: neither is therefore to be despised.

The birth of a pencil (venus)

The chirping swallow call'd forth by the sun . . .
Whose power is this? What god?
—Ben Jonson, *The Vision of Delight*

The Swallow is held sacred to the Gods of the Household and to Aphrodite,
for she also is one of them.
—Aelian, *On the Characteristics of Animals*

When in the field unlettered men had long memories
most of it waste, nettles & briars in hollows
too deep for ploughing

The builders do not know the uses of their building
                              not knowing

THE SOUL'S MISCELLANY

qui ubique est, nusquam est (who is everywhere is nowhere)

I have read many books, but to little purpose for want of good method; I have confusedly tumbled over divers authors in our libraries with small profit for want of art, order, memory, judgement.—*Burton's Anatomy*

We can tell many a feigned tale to look like the truth, but we can, when we will, utter the truth *(Theogony. 26-27)*

The Man who thought he was glass
The man who thought he was butter
The world itself a great box of simples from which to select the remedy
proper to one's own kind of malady
(So that one may be reduced to folding his arms and pulling his hat brim over his face)

Rather than to space we turned in to an implosion
In where our imagined smallness our imagined vanishing
managed great cavities and caverns
This time the trip is around the world and through
the conjectural cosmos. And so forth. And so forth

when one world is taken away
importantly you want someone

we are only that amphibious piece between a corporal and spiritual essence,
that middle form that links those two together
—*Th. Browne (R. Medici)*

ontogeny as phylogeny cosmogeny theogony

Figura verborum
The numerous atoms are in constant motion;
they move about in the void, combine and
repel one another: a dance of figures
a little cake shaped like a boat

my idea—Poetry—kissed the hand
for so long—waiting for someone to do
something—Of these labours
and recreations—some with delight
some within doors, some natural, some artificial
heart-easing mirth and vain deluding joys

sees the moon terrified as one
led astray in the midst of her path
describing his lark abroad by day
observe the trembling poplars from the lawn
and seated at the open window listen
in the stillness for the first song of the nightingale

I have quoted this a curiosity
we see sufficiently furnished
judging chambers changing there
appearances gradually known
they fly, now, in the garden
the annual series of the plants and daily bloom

The Sea ceased from her raging
I went down to the bottoms of the mountains
The waters compassed me about
even to the soul
her bars about me for ever
when my soul fainted
a vehement east wind
it was STE. GABRIEL

About six years ago
he was now in the convent nursing home
Noah sending forth the raven and the dove
The deluge which was played by the Water-Leaders
the wagon was in the form of a ship
with birds and beasts painted on the sides
NOYES FLOOD
The wanton women in their cups
in some heigh place or in the cloudes
it may be God speaketh unto Noe
stanind without the Arke with all his familye
truncated chambers therein thou
the heron and the lemurs
pray on parasols
Roads (WYE) Y on the hill
the ribcage begins a creosote
the Ibyx and the Panther come
spectacled bear, gnu and dromedary
Macaw and ocelot, boar, curlew, widgeon
fox, Now forty 40 dayes are futile gone
Did any of the creatures not ignore

Wolverine, caiman,
emmet, dove

my sweet love brought to me
an olive from some place
and is a sign of peace
All earth dry now I see
this water is away

the sun has rise again
the cormorant, the pelican,
the buck and doe
descending finch ascending curlew's cry
fare well, my darling deere—come quickly come

Notes

behaviour, tumult,
promise cease
obedient immediately
chest ark
brisk, lively ducks
make ready faith
agree
lost mate
mankind
remember
slacken
time

The Dead close their eyes
And if we induce ourselves by May (way?) of Judgement
bound for somewhere from this very statement

That which I have created here
as opposed (in fact) to that which is natural (remains natural)
Occupying an intermediate position
it begins to acquire a soul
having the words to describe itself
at this moment, not sufficiently distanced
from that which makes also myself
absorbing and reflecting recurrently

Our link to the world has already been
one of personal indifference

The model of a child
is enabled to write
that it has no feelings
we assume is correct
unearthed sculptures
were thus seen
as fossil proof
clouds for example
emerge as we
cart before horse
Venus and Mars
in the etching
the man and his toy
are the same order
as is the written
The statue is not
an end in itself
the forms of ruins
a mediating point
the etching of which
in a strict perspective
from which the observer
can be observed

the eye of God
or infinity
the framed picture
of holy relics
giving a soul
to inanimate matter
art has bequeathed
enduring beauty
to the palace of rulers
a man Prometheus
regarding a ring
with diamonds and stones
the prominent globe
clock on a table
such as a compass
a ruler and books
are scattered around
attempts to control
The Kunstkammern

models of buildings
triumphal conveyances
exotic species
of the territory animals

this chain of four limbs
a "Theatre of Memory"
his incunabulum
begins with the story

human salvation
first genealogies
then smiths and clockmakers
three kingdoms of nature
combined of our instruments
the ruling family
portraits of famous coats
jewelry belonging

under the heading
"Indian"costumes
inviting comparison
time-lapse photography
machine driven cosmos
proportioned limbs
pathways for blood
private collection
artistic clockwork
void of all Characters
yet empty cabinet
dark room understanding
represented in pictures
it is impossible
to tell whether nature
created by chance
the ability to move
preparing casts
as they grow in nature
including the lizards
so-called schüttelkasten
landscape with automaton
expressing desire
self-moving engines
with Polyphemus
surrounded by rams
snails as shells
while Galetea
perpetual dolphins
playing the foreground
the weather vane pushing
the wind tower of Athens
Uffizi Tribuna
Académie des Sciences
et des Beaux Arts
infinite collections
aimed at the world
"The city of the Sun"—Campanella
"Tabulae Rudolfinae"—Kepler

Uranienborg
Nova Astronomica

the normal orbits
And terrible danger
since the columns began
already to totter
and threatened cracked walls
Then I set to work
supporting the roof
splendid new timbers
five solid bodies
Urania's Scholars
its unfinished form
Aratus, Hipparchus
Ptolemy and Meton
the cracks in the wall
a four-linked chain
Roman brick columns
hanging from these columns
the domus Salomonis
We have divers clocks
We have a great number
of various motions
Two halls of columns
in Salomon's House
Antiquity offers
a permeable membrane
in Valerius Terminus
we progress to Adam
Paradise Regained
an interminable process
museum of the heavenly
meteors, minerals
the island of Bensalem
transferred into nowhere
these works go beyond
existing creation
I set down at length

his literary work
as a kind of Kunstkammer
the artificialia
the scientifica
the object of nature
And gardens of Palissy
plants from the sun

Bacon's history of erring and varying—which I will suggest is akin to the
monstrous. You might ask if human art (ars) is merely the monstrous—then
why do I continue? Because I must confirm, and continue the monstrous. And
I want to make it. Believing it to be nothing more than its own self—its own
modest enterprise which may be the last growth on this branch or may prove
a limb or a trunk.

The blood dries to sepia
Nature without
fixed direction
until controlled
monstrosities formed
the game of the globe
and the serious joke
a city described
whose buildings harbour
the symbolic ape
who emulates man
rising up to the empyrean
our wondrous strange Theatre
lacking a purpose
"deus ludens"
deliberate disorder
the inventory catalogue
demiurgic production
shells are such monuments
and they shall outlast
even the Pyramids
the Earth be the cabinet
an historical archive
established by language

and natural history
the mental capacity
esoteric images
exoteric language
material change
immutability
admirable fireworks
even of the air
superior modernity
perpetual motion
is nothing to them
the writing Cameralist
departs from an epoch
"On this journey"
forever impressed
the aesthetic has past
now only need
makes demands of our days
impress them to memory
view many things
while still a student
the rosemary heather
image of Andromeda
Andromeda Polifolia
to socialize man
subclasses of flowers
similar to painting
throughout the room
shells in the cornices
The Villa Albani
sol invictus
to sharpen his view
metaphor of growth
blooming and wilting
political freedom
political freedom
in Athens the tyrants
a process the people
distinguished their lands

"the spirit of freedom
was lost from the earth"
and with it play
and with it glory
can still be seen
we follow the masses
of buried sculpture
The Villa Albani
march of the factory
which is unnecessary
sphere of forced movements
not for his own ears
show not the time
life in itself
in order to live
the conclusion of history
to hide the laboratories
stagnate productivity
erection of edifices
surface foundations
the cloaca maxima
manufactures accordingly
prosper most easily
the mind is redundant
aseptic detachment
two realms continue
grace and constraint
most humble presentation
advance marionette
abandoned reflection
rooms filled with mannequins
an effort or person
no obvious purpose
books furnished with structures
metaphoric potential
tabula ansata
"The programmer-god
makes . . . many times over
 . . . the universe proceeds

. . . until it runs down
. . . the slate is wiped clean
. . . a new game is begun"

No one might return

A PASTORAL INTERLUDE

THE ACTS

I'm getting ready. I'm really getting ready
That a kite, the past (future-engine)
should land on the present (future-past/genitals)

The trees drone in their ears
their birds (innumerable)
There to lose what binds us here
no field felt the sky it never fell

no garden alabaster nothing its pure blue
should she live at Kensington or Kew
but every year, when winter came
every summer for seven summers now
she did neither. If she wore pearls, pearls they were
a hundred miles from the sea. A fact that was
lobsters, fresh from lobster pots and salmon and the lobster
they heard dead men they saw a white lady walking under trees
the cook's hands cut cut cut
the room a shell a vase stood in the house
holding distilled across the hall a door opened
the author's last novel was completed just before her death
during the war the action takes place on a single day

Coming from the library the voices stopped in the hall
come earthward a century ago
pleasure's what they want she said you often heard her call
out of the corner of his eye he raised his glass
he saw a flash of white
someone passing silently they
manoeuvred in their water world
made by the trembling grass made by the sky
the ghost of convention rose to the surface
the wall remained nothing but a wall
the tractor has to some extent superseded the plough
the horse had gone but the cow remained
Red Admirals feasting and floating

our part is to be the audience
books open no conclusion come to
and he sitting in the audience
she made another face and dropped the invisible pen
not here not now but somewhere
there was nothing for the audience to do
the flat fields glared the morning room
but we have other lives I think I hope
we live in others we live in things
old men striped trousers girls skin coloured lips
the audience was assembling
spreading across the lawn
and as they took their seats
the human figure seen
to great advantage against
a background of sky
then the play begins

I fear I am not in my perfect mind
the sins I've sinned before cockcrow
Did the plot matter?

She fell back lifeless. The gramophone blared
The idiot scampered in and out
the megaphone announced in plain English: An Interval

As usual her vision escaped her
undressing down in the hollow
where dishcloths in the shadow
made pools of yellow
choked with a toad in its throat
the snake was unable to swallow
the toad was unable to die
a blue-bottle settled
the play keeps running in my head
the path was narrow she was broad
swaying slightly as she walked
the little grapes above then were

wet between bird's claws
Perhaps because we've never met before
and never shall again
the door trembled and stood half open
the audience was assembling
the actors were still dressing up among the bushes
d'you think people change?
clearing out a cupboard
I found my father's old top hat
but ourselves do we change?

figures advanced from the bushes
hooped and draped
entered her dressing room
(Enter carrying a parchment)
(reading)
(aside)
(aloud)
(both speak together)
her mirror and lipstick attended her lips and nose
the gramophone which everybody knows to be perfectly true
while her courses ran and speckled eggs in the warm
hollow lay neighbours dig in cottage gardens and lean
over cottage gates
(she hides behind a tree)
(she reveals herself)
The voice stopped but the voice had seen
(they sang)
whose mouths opened but no sound came out
the whole world was filled with dumb yearning
craves the indulgence of the audience
          (owing to lack of time a scene has to be omitted)
Thank heavens
How right. Actors show us too much
Yes they bore one stiff. Up and down the city road
(he hobbles up and down)
The scene ended
Reason descended from her plinth

the words rose and pointed a finger
yet somehow they felt
how could one put it
a little not quite here or there

                     And so to end the play
Let holy virgins hymn perpetually
as if what I call myself was still
floating unattached and didn't settle
over the tops of the bushes came voices
voices without bodies
the audience was on the move
they kept their distance from the dressing room
it all looks very black
ever since I was a child I've felt
then she began again
it's a good day the day we are stripped naked
A lake it was a lake apparently
there was an interval
(they were rolling up the lake)

Nothing happened
present time ourselves he read
they sat exposed they were neither one thing nor the other
they read it in the programme
o that our human pain could here have ending
real swallows the swallows or martins were they?
I am not in my perfect mind
And the audience saw themselves not whole
by any means but at any rate sitting still
the hands of the clock had stopped at the present moment
it was now ourselves
consider the sheep or faith in love
o we're all the same. take myself now
and the desire for immolation
look at ourselves then at the wall

the first note meant a second the second a third
was that voice ourselves?
we are members one of another
we act different parts but are the same
I caught myself too reflected
as it happened in my own mirror
was that the end?

Nature takes part there was the idiot
we're oracles a foretaste of our own religion
one feels such a fool perhaps one day
thinking differently we shall think the same
by means of which we reach the final
or ourselves the audience
all gone under the leaves
scared by shadows passing
the fish had withdrawn
the lilies were shutting
then something moved in the water
she had a glimpse of silver
the fish had come to the surface
it was unlikely that they would ever meet again
the play was over
swallows skimmed the grass
that had been the stage
the flesh poured over her
the hot nerve wired
what interrupted now she passed
then something rose to the surface
the curtain would rise
what would the first words be
I am the slave of my audience
there would be shelter voices oblivion
and two scarcely perceptible figures
she swallowed
ourselves
did you feel she asked what he said
we act different parts but are the same

yes I answered no she added
both had changed
or that the author came out from the bushes
there were letters
the paper that obliterated the day before
then she found the page where she had stopped
the great square of the open window showed
shadows fell he rose
end of the chapter
left alone together
then the curtain rose. They spoke.

If there is on earth a house with many mansions, it is the house of words

—E.M.Forster, *Anonymity: An Enquiry*

THE SABINE VILLA

THE SABINE FARM

In about 33 B.C. he [Quintus Horatius Flaccus] received from Maecenas the Sabine Farm, situated some twenty-five miles to the northeast of Rome, in the valley of the Digentia, a small stream flowing into the Anio.

Stretching his limbs now
under the green arbute-tree
now by the sacred source
of some gentle stream

deliver us   The tribes of fishes in the elms
til then the haunt of doves
& does swam overwhelmed in flood
fond river-god

A MOMENTARY & SUBSIDIARY CONSIDERATION OF
MILTON'S` L'ALLEGRO & IL PENSEROSO

But the most pleasant of all outward pastimes is
deamulatio per amoena loca (strolling through pleasant scenes)
to walk amongst orchards, gardens, arches, groves, lawns
rivulets in a fair meadow ubi variae avium cantationes
(to enjoy the songs of the birds)
florum colores (colours of the flowers)
pratorum fructices (the verdures of the meadows)

For Dürer's dark sky lit by
a comet and adorned
with lunar rainbow

we have a grateful shade
by day, the steady shining of the Bear by night
Wrapt in a pleasing fit
agreeable & Country-Like

SOME IMITATIONS OUT OF HORACE

We saw the yellow Tiber
battle over battle
Which gods shall we call
to aid the falling empire?

some (there were those/there are whose) only task   some only task
It is to hymn (In unbroken song) the town   to hymn the town
end troubles/life with mellow wine   with mellow wine
the straining woods no longer uphold their burden

the streams are frozen
pile high wood
bring forth the Sabine Jar
the wine four winters old

Busy Thyself with household chores
since life is brief
cut short
far-reaching hopes

Curious his unshorn locks
stern poverty bred war
a farm
angry with polluted groves

★

we have a lesson
fought out to the bitter end
over the festal board
we have a lesson
with furious desire

Here set me up
an altar of verdant turf   a turf altar
here sprays of leaves
a bowl of wine

what makes give up so willingly
the green to whitetell with what wound
what shaft he languishes in bliss
whose inclination falters
whatever passions master thee
you need not blush
a common night awaits
the harvest
tho
I have sworn faith only to myself
and wither without water
I myself, when a worthier person called
was held fast in pale habits
Faith bound with white cloth around the hand

Alas the shame of our scares
& crimes & brothers dead
what wrong have we not touched
the ivy chokes the oak

blare of thorns our ears
I already seem to hear
fires hidden under ashes
even now the clear sounds

take holiday in wine some
too brief blossoms
and youth allow
you leave all purchased land
your house the yellow Tiber washes
what Nothing is inherits
and beneath the canopy of trees
our future ash inhabits

Having fallen in love I go back to my life. This makes both bearable

*

Happy enough in my Sabine farm
the grave lends an ear to free the poor man
I shall quit the towns of men
Even now the winter gathers over my shoulder

When if not now
an old man takes a lover
her grilled and rippled front
his dugs and both commit in upward struggle

as focused frenzied out of focus
young abstracted foxes animals
his elbowed member polished
to her leather

(he apologizes later for fellating younger men)
immortal natures have immortal sorrows
yet if we mortals are unhappy
death is the harbour from our quarrels troubles

★

quiet boy
I am in love with loving him
or being his soft voice
of poetry outside the school

Ceres of the yellow hair
it is no pity that you eat a lamb
it is a celebration
such as when you become the same

my darling boy has sunken down
into a quarry pond—marl pool
his limp limbs slowly yellow
under a still rippled shallow

A free adaptation
and now one is in the other's arms
it won't end here
in the bath house—unused
a city trembles falling horses
Eumolpus the poet in poor garb
black eels—oars in water

FUVK BY CKCK5V

IMITATIONS OF HORACE (KEATS)

Why should I change my Sabine dale
whatever limit bounds the world
I here am strayed through hallowed groves
and overcome with sleep
at last alone
the burden of this living done
I climb my lofty Sabine hills or
In Hampstead to the Vale of Health
struck down with the descending bolt
the forests of his native isles, Apollo's Self
bidden by some peddler or the captain of some hidden-sail
at nightfall close your dwelling
gaze into the streets of music, cruel

and keep the lamps alight till dawn
the present hour abandon serious things
less stable than the tossing cork
the wild boar lurking in the thick-set copse
the dark red blossom of the rose

I seek the camp of those desiring
naught to hide within my barns
a beggar in the midst (of mighty wealth)
my stream of pure blest water
him who's given just enough
tomorrow's tempest from the east

with many leaves the grove
the shore with useless (sea)weed
your soul with wine
a pig but two months old

in summer I am my desire
cooling his shoulders in the breeze
when dire need nails deep

a screaming lapwing brought down from the fields/ as a prophetic augur,
nothing in the night/ except the stars & waves/ open to me in your palest
blue/—everybody wants you—even you—hair wet and wet where hair has yet
to grow

erstwhile among the meadows absolved in flowers
with a hundred cities for the first time
crying it happens once for the first time
darkling sea the shores with shock
Europa entrusted to the bull
by frenzy overmatched
a single death an idle leg
closest to his victim in experience

★

the wet bank I shall not die altogether
on and on from low to high estate
the wasting rain yet part of me shall grow

·I am not as I was
belly pushed out hair & eyes dull
an eloquent youth with nothing to account

a moth calls
who will be the next man?
with every word
your mediocrity

the grass returning (New York)
the horse became a slave
born to eat and work
cutthroats get up at night to cut men's throats

I am gone away to hide someplace
no longer asking of the crowd
your monster has many heads
many ears and many mouths

willing and unwilling animals
what if the English People ask me why?
I'll emulate myself
your monster has a hundred forms

I have a jar full in my garden
parsley ivy
bending back the hair
the house

bidden go home I went my way
irresolute
hard on my course
with long hair gathered in a knot

indomitable cosmetic heart
has laid down in a field
A House, its torso in a field
the doves descend upon

IMITATIONS OF HORACE (KEATS)

The local Genius hurries me aloft
One there surely was
('The Wizard of the North')
Or Sabine vales explored inspire a wish
To meet the shade of Horace by the side
Of his Bandusia's fount; or I invoke
His presence to point out the spot where once
He sate, and eulogized with earnest pen
Peace, leisure, freedom, moderate desires;
And all the immunities of rural life
Extolled, behind Vacuna's crumbling fare . . .

—Wordsworth *Memorials of A tour in Italy* 1837

For while by Chloë's image charm'd
Too far in Sabine woods I stray'd;
Me singing, careless and unarm'd,
A grizly wolf surprised, and fled . . .

—Samuel Johnson, *first version of Horace Bk I. Ode xxii*

See how the whatever remained of Man
by clouds by rain is veil'd a song
I pierce the Clouds

I am not now
as in the sound
of your soft animal
too fierce Mother
turning will to fires

His house embosom'd in the Grove
Sacred to social life and dreams
The Thames or Avon burning close
A self-tormentor in the shadow
of a passing glint

A cirl bunting quiet on the wire
very rare are talking animals
sometimes men are said to come from trees
(kykeõn)
(electrum)

(Except a corn of wheat fall into the ground and die,
it abideth alone; but if it die,
it bringeth forth much fruit   *John* 12:24)

(A mortal ripens like corn
and like corn is born again
—*Katha Upanishad*)

that she had a gift for singing
was tall and yellow-haired
she died neglected and was buried
near the yellow Tiber

(thoughts of morality,
of right and wrong
ways to get a livelihood
and of the land—robbed from the poet—
never given back)

Our genuine admiration of a great poet is a continuous undercurrent of feeling! It is
everywhere present, but seldom anywhere as a separate excitement
—S.T.C. *Biographia Literaria* p.12

I retired to a cottage in Somersetshire at the foot of Quantock and devoted my thoughts
and studies to the foundations of religion and morals. Here I found myself all afloat.
—ibid. p103

★

A body in motion not in motion
air articulated into nonsense
send me my brother home I can no longer
bear the weight I am to bear

such self-sown odes
such stresses what means
less than nothing to a modern audience
the ashes, the grand elms & cypresses
while the Villa farm was being built
the locks & gates the cuttings
sidings bridges tow path
picked from the ground

a garden of necessity
precise English equivalent
a death scene which occurs uniquely
episodes under the walls

the formal clang
if it had not been
written it would have
been unimaginable

spoken by messengers
they describe elsewhere
hardly speak at all
no longer bear the intrusions

and what appeared was not
fulfilled unlikely (and) that was how
the text was fixed by being written down
and learnt by heart

the poem is just a patch
of sunlight moving over grass
over a breathing field
details of plot we uncover

we cannot find for example
a real object with properties
atoms and void as conventions
the truth is unavailable

★

I have my Horace with me

★

sweet is the swallow sound
but sweet aswell the boy
Asked for they come for me
bearing me away

The head of Orpheus was tombed at Antissaia
and there the nightingales sang most divine
a bird had but to perch upon a tomb
her song became a miracle / her song is wine

Audience withdraw into yourselves
the heat rises from the lawn
lifts the head outside the house
I cannot think only the trees remain

Many would-be doctors were compelled
to move away from home
In August 1810 (1812)
apprenticed to another doctor, boyhood over

It might be I have nothing I can say
the hands flapping awkwardly

here to improve without audience
presently we know everything there is to know

amidst a flood of papers
I heard the voices rise

the sitting room-cum-study
overlooked a pretty avenue of limes

which led on to the Heath
this far-famed island comprehending as it does

chasms and convulsions
cultivated plains / wooded seclusions

It was a hideaway and vantage point
and also the surrounding world

a sonnet of reproach an exhortation
habit (has) made me a Leviathan.

the practice of pismires & bees
a man may carry his own pyre

There was not a soul? about
whom one might have asked the way

Reading of canals—I went to college in Victorian Suburbia
what are we waiting for—cupboards under stairs
cheap wardrobes where the second hands collect
Stanley Spencer painted my portrait
Earl's Court sharing blankets with the cat—Rochester drawing rooms
Green china
Ombersley courtship
Porcelain peartree

KEATS'S HOUSE & THE SABINE VILLA

I am separated from you . . .
Give my love to both houses   *Tuesday, Hampstead, 1818*

former lodgings at the Burrough
enquiries after you particularly
"Souls of poets dead & gone &c."
The Wednesday before last Shelley
& I wrote a sonnet on the River Nile
"The two-and-thirty Pallaces"
A doze upon a sofa does not hinder it
Man should whisper to his neighbour
a democracy of forest trees
let us open up our leaves
budding patiently
I have not read any Books
I had no Idea but Morning
(Shelley cast his features on the water)

{Poetry} should strike the Reader as a wording of his own highest thoughts, and
appear almost a Remembrance   *Hampstead 27 Feby*

Remember me to Percy Street
I escaped being blown over and blown under
trees & houses & being toppled on me
I want to forget it and make my mind free for something new

What a happy thing it would be
if we could settle our thoughts
make our minds up on any matter
in five minutes and remain content
that is to build a sort of mental Cottage
of feelings quiet and pleasant

Who would live in the region of Mists
there is something else wanting
to someone who passes his life among books

it is impossible to know how far knowledge
will console us for the death of a friend
I compare human life to a large Mansion
of Many Apartments
We are not the balance of good and evil
We are in a Mist
I may have read these things before
After all there is certainly something real in the World
remember me to all The Leaves
have been out here for MONY a day

I have not an idea to put on paper
my hand feels like lead
and yet it is an unpleasant numbness
it does not take away the pain of existence

I don't know what to write—Monday
I am troubling you with Moods of my own mind
or rather body—for the mind there is none

I could not feel comfortable
making sentences for you
I am your debtor
like the swallow sleeping on its wing
the world has something else to do
Perhaps if my affairs were in a different state
Life must be undergone
it depends upon a thousand Circumstances
I am not at Home
If I take any book with me
I want to read you I should much like to read it there for you

Here beginneth my journal, this Thursday, 1818
for there is no such thing as time and space
and I am writing at this present
What can we say?
I live in the eye
We shall see

I'll write you on my word the first
and most likely the last I ever shall
what shall it be about?
I have slept and walked
drop like a Hawk on some letters from you
This is all[…] in the m[…] please a[…]
I am a day behind
I wrote a note & left it on the Mantelpiece
This is what I like better than scenery
I fear our continued moving from place to place
we are mere creatures of Rivers, Lakes
old whitewashed narrow streets
broad red brick ones more modern
where we shall linger
the clouds, the Sky, the Houses
plenty of wretched Cottages
my coat has gone
my fellow traveler
through Summer & Autumn

(I'll not run over the Ground we have passed
One of the pleasantest means of annulling self
is approaching such a shrine as the Cottage
I would always find an eggshell for Melancholy)

I cannot write about scenery
you would rather read Horace afterwards
then remember yourself

My sensations are sometimes deadened for weeks together
I have been getting more and more close to you every day
having a scrap of paper pasted in the book he sent
two dead eternities
another cannot wake thy giant size

We lost our way yesterday

I had determined to write a sonnet in the Cottage
I wrote some lines cousin-german to the Circumstance
we are now in by comparison a Mansion-One

I will tell you exactly where we are
sometimes appearing as one Lake
I have been no where else except to Wentworth place

AN ENQUIRY INTO THE SITUATION AND
CIRCUMSTANCES OF HORACE'S SABINE VILLA

Horace, the prince of Roman poets was possessed of a villa in the Sabine

teaching us in every line of every book
In a word he labours
graceful negligence
tranquil retirement (reticence)
which we imitate with a backwards glance

delicacy in colouring and insight
Ovid himself in his Erato
depicted in one mural
that might have set M on his travels
to Horace's villa
eminent painter renowned for his abilities in all the noble arts
enfeebled scholar-painter
even as he sketched the monuments of Rome
a site at once real and of the imagination
give nothing a local habitation
topography idealized at the dinner-party
where Horace loved and drank cool wine
some ruins fell on knees uttered some enthusiastic words
to the Licenza Valley and the Sabine Hills
Unable to contain himself, in the end buildings are destroyed
and ruins disappear

The landscape actual
in Pope's Horatian Imitations
where the Latin faced the English
actual lacunae where
Horace's weak health
racked with Sciatics Martyr'd with the stone
rented accommodation at Twickenham
remember that a farm is like a man
a cathedral of trees—an obelisk commemorating
In the absence of reliable remains
how to translate Horace in his own landscape

a landskip given significance
by the words printed under it

far from specific far from precise
the great utility of how a Roman lived
was that it afforded scope for imitation
gardens, patches, orchards, vines
praise of locality
attention to topography or Horace's lines . . .

*(You will read him with more enthusiasm than elsewhere; you will imagine you see the
philosophic poet wandering among the groves
—John Moore, A View of Society and Manners in Italy, 1781*

*If you ever come to Tivoli . . . be sure to put Horace in your Pocket
—Ibid.*

*Higher up among the mountains, Horace had his little farm which he seemed to enjoy so much
. . . This Country, like that of the Latin's seems formed in a peculiar manner by Nature for the
Study of the Landscape-Painter.
—Thomas Jones, 1777*

Temple of Apollo, *William Woollett, after Claude Lorraine, 1760*
Jacob More, View near Horace's Villa, *1777*
View of Horace's Villa, *Rocca Giovane,*
Jakob Philipp Haskert (engraved by Luigi Sabatelli), Licenza Series, *1780*
Louis Ducros, Site of Horace's Villa, *1793-4*

Biondo's Italia Illustrata
Chiverius's Italia Antiqua
The Maire-Boscovich maps of Latium)

. . . all giving rise to an image of the house as an hanging garden
raised above the ground, set in a Virgilian dream
cultivated about with most excellent fruits
loggias made in all four fronts
pausing while ascending the ramp

a little like the paintings of Carpaccio
a babbling spring nearby, a pool moss bordered, and a rill
ghosting through the grass

the sequence of rooms, the dining room lightly washed
a view through the inner-hall
the courtyard with two colonnades
shaded by four plane trees and
then suddenly in the midst of this
what looks like a real piece of rural countryside
scented with violets, haunting the marble
the evening clicking slowly in still heat
thought is placed in the vestibulium
then the atrium, around the impluvium
to the cubicula and the exedrae
I will describe for you in rambling style
the pattern of his letters
the veins of glittering marble
each chamber with its windows
its own particular sea
training memory
a name will lend authority
that he named each room
the wall-paintings taking as their subject
harbours, temples, groves
cattle, shepherds and the wanderings of Ulysses
I am now writing a book
the text, with all associations
that is, landscape
coalesces to a whole

THE SEARCH OR QUEST

there is no satisfaction
anyway desire for what one lacks
becomes a habit of possession
this is a monument
broken off another monument

I want to read again
myself over again
& over
House of that era

say
300 year old farm
windows & replaced furniture
original structure

The passage that concerns us makes this knot
dissolves like the reflections of Narcissi
on the water as the pupil of the eye
whose ever forming shape wells in alterity

RUINE DELLA VILLA D'ORAZIO

Baron de Saint'Odile
~~Plenipotentiary to the Holy See~~
~~of his Majesty the Emperor and Grand Duke of Tuscany~~
~~persuaded that the Villa was located in Licenza~~
~~having~~ observed the remains of an ancient structure
~~under a spring from which without doubt~~
~~the stream of Licenza takes it name~~
he imagines Horace's House once here
~~and undertakes its scavamento~~
~~There a pipe is also seen~~
~~bringing water from this spring~~
~~both for domestic use and also, perhaps~~
~~for the convenience of a domestic bath~~

Abbé De Chaupy ~~having combed the area~~
& wrote ~~a work in several volumes arguing~~
~~that when Horace speaks of his own house~~
~~he speaks of the Digentia, Mons Lucretilis~~
~~& of the Sabine Valleys where one has~~ to find
a conclusion to argument and travels.

PREFACE TO M'S ENQUIRY

North of Vicovaro
between Rocca Giovine
and Licenza. An unknown amanuensis
copied his last draft
making what was possibly fair copy

M had maps on his mind
he traveled south through Albano
Nemi and Velltri to the Pomptine marshes
Terracina, ultimately Naples
Using Tivoli as a base
staying at Signor Cochimara's house
Who's gardens clothed the Temple of the Sibyl
& thence to the Count Orsini
out of each window views of the valley
and after dinner we went together
to see Horace's country House
of which there is very few remains

AN ENQUIRY &C.

remarkable for the purity of its air
not unfit for both philosopher and poet
ask not if his farm maintains
with fruits and grains
Around its Bridegroom-Elm
its loquacious stream
the Sun on either side
the Cattle led a soft retreat
all parts relative to the whole
a close valley in the midst of hills
The Emperor Vespasian restored a Temple here
to Victory ruined by age
a lurking place a traveler may pass
his whole life without seeing this
there is a strong curiosity in man
to know the personal circumstances of the past
without enquiring strictly into useful tendency
of this sort of curiosity
it is sufficient to say
(in its defence it is a part of human nature)
new lights will be from thence
reflected on his poetry
his small farm
the small field that restores me to myself
It is a most singular spot of ground
for musing on my lovely maid
the valley is so deep in shade
never to feel the rays of noon
except around the solstice
mistress of the lyric string
Careless like a Bride
To Thee I consecrate the pine
which nodding waves my Villa round
Fonte Bello, Fonte Ratini
An hundred lowing Kine
And scorn the crowd
By this we learn that Horace had

as Villa but his Sabine one
Some readers have imagined
that the poet was deliberating change
What should I, a bachelor, need
what do the flowers mean
some meat some wine
A Goat upon the Shrine
I know not how to reconcile this seeming inconsistency
to live and stay

turning the ground through which it formerly ran clear
into a sort of bog
getting rid of the fountain itself
turning a mill
which he intended to erect
Such has been the fate of Fons Bandusiae
buried it alive it will
run forever in the smooth detail
of its description

Horace was by birth a Venusine
an accidental residence
Tomorrow you will be presented with a kid
with Incense and a ravening Swine
To now appease the Household Gods
The Preservation of his Home, his Odes.
Where a devoted Tree will fall
While Noise & Quarrels shall be done
Worshipped in common by all country folk
having invoked Diana she must come
the fountain I have described is in the Straight
road from Rome to Brundusium
I often wished I had a farm
A garden Where
My Parsley Crowns were spread
The Gardens you enjoy
a spring of never failing water near my house
besides a little ancient Grove
Running down aslant the hill

it passes near the ruins of his house
crossing the highway
a little to the north
the former Counts Orsini
made a cascade (to be) found
between the ruins of two ancient homes
preserved in the name of an Hermitage
(L'Ermitaggio della Case)
a mosaic of very elegant foliage
a late discovery of leaden pipes
While careless in the woods I strayed
and likewise found an altar to Jupiter
used by a peasant in Licenza to hold water
for his chickens. But the letters
which have not suffered are distinct
Vacuna equivalent to Minerva
to Diana, to Ceres and Bellona
a dedicated tree is down
and all these others grown
the precise situation of the temple may not be ascertained
I carry stones or break the stubborn soil
I am engaged in an enquiry
The houses might still be in-habited
some nights furnished with a feast
The Master leaves another takes his place
with busy haste, with Girls and Boys
All sort of fruits grow here
The chain of hills divided by the rising day
The last time I was upon this spot
bodies of water running thus
I found there was no town there of that name
so vain possession
I have never had an opportunity
(confirming this observation)
Something more certain and more precise may still be learned
so that when we took our leave
we did with much regret

KEATS

I am at present alone at Wentworth Place   *—Letter, Dec 1818*

The sense of darkness coming over me
I eternally see her figure eternally vanishing
during my last nursing at Wentworth Place
Is there another life? Shall I awake and find all this a dream?
A sudden stop to my life in the middle of one of these letters
would be no bad thing   *—1820*

my mind is a tremble, I cannot tell what I am writing   *—1819*

Suppose me in Rome—well I should see you in a magic mirror   *—1820*

upon which I immediately left Mortimer Terrace   *—1820*

My imagination is a monastry
On Hampstead Heath—I am returning
this morning ~~in bed~~ the matter struck me
in a different manner
We are in a calm and I am easy
and used to keep my eyes
fixed on Hampstead all day
Where can I look for consolation
I have an habitual feeling of my real life having past
Yet I ride the little horse
I should have left

Walthamstow, Winchester, Windermere, Westminster
Teignmouth, Kentish Town, Margate, Milan
Pisa, Oxford, Rome, Chichester
Cheapside, Devonshire, Hampstead, Iona
Ireland, Isle of Wight, Ayr, Bedhampton,

Craven Street, The Swan & Hoop
Ponders End near Enfield
Babbacombe Bay
Bolton-le-Sands
Brentford in Bedhampton The Cap and Bells
Bunhill Fields, City Road
Burton-in-Kendal, Carisbrooke Castle
Kenwood House, Church Street Edmonton
Newgate Street London
recommends Margate
Clerkenwell
Coach and Horses nr the Strand
Field Manor Enfield
French Revolution
Devonshire, Hampshire, Berkshire, Kent
Harrow School, Highgate, Holborn, Margate
Lancaster, Windermere, Derwent, Land's End
Lisbon, London Bridge
Oriel House, Nottingham
Paddington, Plymouth
Redbourne near St.Albans
St. Bartholomew's Somerset
The Swan with Two Necks
Tooley Street, Wentworth Place
Walthamstow, Wentworth Place
Waterloo, Westmorland
Winchester, Yarmouth
Vale of Health, Westminster
Wentworth Place, Hampstead

The Fishponds they visited together
three lyrics tense with sexual desire
Laboriously on a narrow ledge
it was in effect two semi-detached houses
a white regency box
the recently built villa
and in half of which he lived
Jeremy Taylor under his arm
Burton's Anatomy living with Brown

came close to touching
that lay ahead of him
In the days before leaving
two sitting rooms-cum-studios
wine cellar, kitchen
tall ground floor windows
a plum-tree a mulberry tree
a compact pretty white painted house
a hedge of Laurustinus
the well tended garden
The dream he told
I floated about
even flowery tree tops sprung
one of the most delightful
ever had in my
Within a few moments
refusing to see
far from Arcadia
~~Ode to a Nightingale~~
collect his belongings
returning to College Street
finished Bright Star
returning from Winchester
speech day at Westminster
trivial incidents
wretchedly furious
until he began
late summer began
when he returned
to Wentworth Place
he had departed
is present to me
the cost of the journey
Within a short space of time
now part of history
leaves to a tree

NONSUCH PALACE

Her Majesty is returned again to Nonsuch
which of all places she likes best

the chief ornament, eclipse and glory of its kind
All places full of Kings, Caesars, Sciences, Gods

A shining column carries of a snow-white nymph
whose leaden breasts flow jets into the ivory marble

full of concealed pipes which spirt upon
the dream-like Alice crouching artfully

So that one would inevitably
take them for real ones

Three Graces arms entwined
The cobbled yard was crossed with flags

one tower, a clock, a symphony
six gilded horoscopes a very special ornament to Nonesuch House

To Henry's right hand
the façade of his own apartments

bewildering symbolic plaster females
thirty-one (Roman) Emperors from Caesar to the brutish Aemilianus

florid architecture turns his eyes
he will say that it easily bears off the prize

such are its paintings, gilding, decoration of all kinds
that you would say that it is the sky spangled with stars

a masquerade where she could hide away
the gift and private dance

However it is possible to reconstruct
Her Majesty is returned again to Nonsuch

Enter the outer court there was inevitably a maze
an orchard haphazard a man-made wilderness

delicious song of birds in trees planted along the sides
shrubs and plants (sown) in intricate circles

the same flamboyant idiom set forward on her head
a bird of Paradise seeming no more than twenty years of age

a lavish place of nonsense, coursing and hunting
in the great deer park in his significance

ripping its belly open, putting his hands and sometimes feet inside
stripped Nonsuch of its furniture—a ship named after his estate

I supped in Nonesuch House, took an exact view
statues and bassrelievos, punctuations of the outside walls of court

A great walke of an elme and a walnutt set
one after another in order

I walked, also, into the ruined garden
The ways, very bad, and the weather worse

It was pulled down and crumbled on its own
a shell used for mixing cosmetics, traces of rouge still visible

Three popinjays, a perfume bottle, chamber pots
Tudor roses made of lead like nothing else on earth.

FIELD NOTES

During summer evenings over London gardens
hosts of swallows, swifts and martins
congregate to chase ~~the~~ insects risen
hundreds of feet above the lawns—their wheeling
shrieks and whistles floating down
to a thousand open windows ~~in the still~~ below
~~Silver light~~

~~A thousand listeners lifted~~
— William Williamson, *Journals*

Libertà ! molto e desiato bene! I revolved these words in my heart on the great plaza of
Turin, where we never wearied of watching the flight of innumerable swallows, hearing a
thousand little joyous cries. On their descent from the Alps they found numerous convenient
habitations all prepared for their reception, in the apertures left by the scaffold-beams in the
very walls of the palaces. At times, and frequently in the evening, they chattered very loudly
and cried shrilly, to prevent us from understanding them . . . Unlike man who is incessantly
called back to earth, they seem to gravitate above. Never have I seen the image of a more
sovereign liberty.
—Jules Michelet, *A reminiscence of Turin.*

Sept. 22: Swallows abound, Tops of the beeches are fringed with yellow. This morning
the swallows rendezvoused in a neighbour's wallnut tree. At the dawn of day they arose
altogether in infinite numbers occasioning such a rushing with the strokes of their wings
as might be heard to a considerate distance, [Note inserted later]. Since that no flock has
appeared, only some late broods, & stragglers.
—Gilbert White, *Naturalist's Journal*, 1771

Furze lark   Shunning a shower   Mavis   The Swallow building
Under the arch   Swordly well   stone pits   The sand Martin
—John Clare, *A Note, taken from a scrap of paper.*

The Soul is alien to the body, a nightingale to the air, a swallow in an house.

—Robert Burton, *Anatomy of Melancholy;*
Remedies Against Discontents

SOUL

HOUSE

During WW 2 the poet William Williamson worked as a radio operator on a remote Hebridean island. A series of poetic fragments and long prose pieces were later found written on the walls of his weaver's cottage.

animals with a broader spectrum of vision, such as the squirrel, such as the rabbit, have a different sense of interiority. there is little behind their eyes

Age 36. Eat a cooked egg for breakfast

And for them survival is based on accepting interaction exteriority is a priority.

A machine extends the surface of the body. speaking through a machine is in kind no further from the self than speaking through your mouth the voice is the first machine of the self we feel distanced from. We are our hands differently than our voice.

The inside of the body is the same order of existence as the outside. Through fear we privilege the unobserved. The self is a machine. If we do not believe a car speaks for us.

Soul is the idea that man exists in a 'profound' sense
beneath the surface, in existence I gauge
depth is an illusion a metaphysicalized desire
for individual presence perhaps understanding
the impersonality of language but nonetheless
If soul exists anywhere it is during language
during the word soul during the word word for that matter
it is real I see it written
(or metaphor for everything we actually spoken)
might be one something to the prehistoric caves
word as sight
the dimensions of My head
but I see only not in
a scratch on the surface
along the skin
This wall is my soul

This wall is

Soul is the idea that man exists in a 'profound' sense
beneath the surface, in existence I gouge[2]
depth is an illusion a metaphoricalized desire
for individual presence perhaps understanding
the impersonality of language but nonetheless
If soul exists anywhere it is during language
during the word soul during the word word for that matter
it is real I see it written
(our metaphors for occupancy are naturally spatial)
might it owe something to the protective caves
around our eyes
the dimensions of the head
but I see out not in
a creature on the surface
along the skin
This wall is my soul
This wall is W . . . m W . . . . on [illegible autograph]

---

[2] pencil marks particularly deep here

Is the inscription by the subject (poet) of the subject (house) on the object (house) by the object (poet) indication of unity? Immanence? No—the act of poetry is acknowledgement of separation. The need to write is the due process of the distraught inhabitant within the house. Unacknowledged inhabitance is separation. Acknowledged inhabitance is separation challenged in the moment. The house has made him what he is, it is no matter that he has just arrived. you and your home are coeval.

The countenance of the house
acknowledged in its symmetry
windows door describes us
as a bird branches

I seem to see a dream of boards
of a once occupied unoccupied hall
where I remember my own occupancy
looking for some fragments in the floor
where I sometimes wake and sometimes walk

somnambulantia
partial decay of hall feathers
recreate arena
shutters part together

the realm of the physical and the realm of the imaginary are both worlds

floods brown flares sodium
proscenium and stalls
the set rehearsals
here something is wanting

you wont believe it everything is useful
the world is for you
okay here it is
I'm cutting my blood up to here

one moment for example
up from the fishing pools nr Ombersley Court
a tree in dramatic clarity
exactly

I talked with you in a dream
why does the swallow (wake?) me
who sings and (tongueless) cannot sing
who wheezes level with my (window) waking

The Garden shall be observed from this dwelling
a small plot from the windows roughly cultivated
for ornament the wild graves (grass) of the region and
such as fern some lilies, poppies and dog rose
In ornament and production a walnut & a cherry
having no inclination or means I have no lawn
but a beach pebble pathway which widens to serve
as my dining area
the soil is good heavy & well drained
potatoes ash or rabbits

consciousness is the unending task my reason
and excuses pleasures are the shape
of my continuing complexity describes
one simple fact. unavoidable. Satis superque

I have been wearing the blue sky
of course the water without building
being this alone I'm everything
the still sea is green algae

a white shirt will not last
your feet dangle a piece of music cannot last
light won't the street the Cathedral
everything will almost safety caring accurate inevitably

I travel through the corpse of another
breathing from organ to organ
as one visits a city minding
one's head at the low ceilings

(The World that I regard is myself; it is the microcosm—Sir Thomas Browne)

I cannot but conjecture this to be the reason
the mind—the highest sort—imagination—prophets
they that, most of them are poor, they find their minds
with their own flights that they neglect the study of the floor

and those ecstatic souls do walk about in their own corpses
til waking kills us daily hourly minutely
whereby we live a middle death and middle life
a band of cloud along horizon hills

This one edge these many cliffs

we sit down with a book
we lie down my friend and I
and the book open reading
we are holding our breath against each other
ourselves shuddering with pulse
apart from ourselves—the concentration
touching where we both are

The line moves the point along in two dimensions. With the acceptance of the fragment the outside of the poem's event is indicated simultaneously—it becomes three-dimensional. Now, in this poetry of fragment after fragment we experience more than just the poem and its outside, we experience the simultaneity of many poems, all poems, with their own ends and their beginnings—their readings—intersecting—their lives in the space of being read—on the page just now we see self-consciously noted a fourth-dimensionality.

The page indicates poems moving and arriving.

The space of the poem is blown open like the body is blown open.

We collect ourselves by collecting the world. It is a visualized model of the processes of the mind, as we wish to enter the forbidden chambers of the self.

The dream of interiority is man's slow acceptance of the distancing caused by self-conscious ex-istence. It is a quick circuit built to bridge that space between what is and what was thought. Without consciousness or without language (the vehicle between world and idea of self in world) we might not need to see our eyes as separate from that which we see. We might understand "self" as a fourth-dimensional view over the three dimensional world.

We say 'here is the world.' In the lyric poem we say "here I am"—in the hope, perhaps, that this address will indicate directly—so that language need not offer an alternative to the trace of the body—but every utterance is an immediate divergence—and every telling is of something other than the self. But it is of the body, it is of the body.

To imagine the self simply located behind the eyes is to imagine the word made flesh (which is the project of religion, the job of relocating the self in an alternative authority). When I say "here I am" I might as well mean the blanket I sit on or the window I am not looking through. The mouth is no cloaca laying existence. Break open an egg and it reveals an egg. The inside of the body is simply there for protection—it is not hiding anything we might imagine to be a self—when we die—that which departs was the least thing, most commonly worn and easily shared—when we die that which we call soul departs even more easily than a breath—it is a word said that cannot stay with us.

Swallow, I also seek and do not find
— Sydney Dobell

What exile from his country ever escaped himself as well?
— Horace, Ode XXXIV

Writing is the ceaseless repetition of what cannot be grasped
before which the I loses its ipseity (Levinas). The poet works
before the inexhaustible language—a vast ocean, each word a
movement in this direction or that—a narration of exile—the self
annihilated and each word cast off indifferently . . . swallowed.
There is no home—there is only searching.
— William Williamson

JOURNAL (HOME)

Moving Backwards

I am constantly remembering that I have not stopped loving
any of them, for any of the reasons we were together or apart

I fortified my heart and braced myself to enter England
It was lovely to see you all—laid out gardens and
heroic trees. When I closed my eyes to the watery . . .

I can keep my euphoria going because of these trees
propped up on these trees.

The difficulty has been to remain myself (for me to enjoy) so far
away from home. Occasionally, lost in enthusiasm or work this was so
And occasionally, as this morning, a hummingbird hovers over the trumpet vine
and of course it is a miracle.

The thunderous galloping hare

Within your heart a little spirit moved and came out from your eyes and came to wound me as I was gazing on your loveliness and made its way through my eyes so quick . . . that it put heart and soul to sudden flight. . . . Then when the soul had been restored a little, it called out to the heart, "Are you dead, then? For I don't feel you in your proper place!"

When I am not looking—when I do not look
or see you as you are today in Green felt hat
and red your favourite colours saying look at me

again I remember you unseen
shadows under mounds cloth gathered
in hair-light brown brown flickering
limbs at the elbow limbs at the graceful folded
fingers then prick themselves unravel
and eventually this gown discovered
for small inched victory slapped down

we have negotiated a non-peace for ourselves

I was recognized by one who took me by the skirt and cried
(This means of course no disrespect) There can be no comeliness in limbo
And yet here in its very desolation and unsubmissive life
I had in plenty what I wanted, now, alas, look and attend this water
waited for Last season's fruit is eaten last season I wanted
      Of course there are dissimilarities as well
      tin, asphalt, pail, What! are you here?
      the dramatized encounter of the wholly world
      whose very unexpectedness and 'unreality' releases
      generally unspoken but entirely urgent cares
      In a word, the meeting never is a meeting
      A crowd, over the medieval bridge
      establishing relationships between the medieval and the modern world
      apparently implied (Can you say for sure that it is not?)

I almost wish I could have hung about outside so as to be able to write about this place I was arriving at. . . . I am able to do a bit of planning ahead before birth . . . to have whole days in front of one in which one can see how far one can reach into that unknown realm . . . but the perch that just oneself provided was not enough for other than retaining some sense of home & real being.

and full of pike and tench among the weeds
and under the tall water
docks and willow herbs
not knowledge, not
wisdom, given to mysterious
average man who answers
and thrushes hardly leave the corn
A dream has passed silent of wing no sound
from cottages The dreams are over them
satisfactions, consolations, hopes
You see we have been happy
in common and in secret
one feels how wonderful it would be to be
just where one is.

We wish to prolong what we can see and touch and talk of
We can do the work of the Universe
though we shed friends and country
house and clothes and flesh and are invisible

We just make empty handed armless snatches in the air
& catch our love everywhere and it is marvelous
that longing never dies & one can't improve one's vision
even the fool's about the business of eternity
those that move about outside
they are also of our company

The coombes breed whole families
daintiest snails in saxifrage & moschatel
the spurge and spurge laurel
saffron-hearted primrose greenish in the light of its own leaves

Now and In England
by the last boat leave
radiant with otherness
a thin continuance

my heart is congested by glittering on a glistening quince tree—my ribcage has splintered through a lung. Such is teaching. And I cannot teach with nothing below me but debris. This not grandiose. My daughters are upon me the reckless victims of neglect and puerile indecency. I have not trained my indecency. It describes only laziness and inadequacy. If I were to follow truthfully truthfully my desires nothing could be indecent.

I never shook off the feeling that something very obvious, very manifest in itself was hidden from me.
—W. G .Sebald, *Austerlitz*

My life is a hesitation before birth
—Franz Kafka, *Diaries*

In reading I had thought the words inside my head—that sounds were in my ear—but noticing today the words 'at Alexandria, with the founding of the museum and its library' the words themselves held the site of the sound. The halls of Alexandria must have been silent—with a thousand heads listening to the silent page expound.

We who dwell on Earth can do nothing of ourselves
—William Blake

Why don't we make some new emotions
—Alice Notley

A huge, plunging, tremendous soul. I would like to be a tree for a while. The great lust of roots. Root-lust. And no mind at all.
—D. H. Lawrence

the trees outlive us disappear
the horse are execute
are hanged above the earth
their legs so long yet cannot reach

(I had forgotten my dream of owning an orchard)
(One need not own an olive grove)

not writing I am the whole universe. that is I do not exist separately

One should have the faith to write transparently
but is continually pulled by the desire to write
this desire this vanity to show this memorial to self
is where the weak self encroached or the healthy self encroaches
transparency would live for ever
But of the idea, wanting to own its excitement
when the next and then the next
I congratulate myself, walking is not flying
an awkward upright creature / creator projected by jerks
accident after accident I try to own
I've started I've begun
If I had the faith to live transparently I would not eat
I would not need to bury here my shit
again and again to be found

have you written this as an appeal
to drag the corpse from the vultures
back inside the city wall
the author sniffing his own future
police time wasted by innocent confessors
testing the ground before the fall

to note the towers of umbelliferae
attend the thrill of presence
vanished wren the self
surfeited to an ecstasy
authentic glory must translate
that this survive
the urgent voice believed its correspondence to reality
Anyone who couldn't see, Anyone deaf
how swamped in certainty
the painter attempts the literal
and yet time after time
the way he puts paint on gives way

Monday

You can achieve nothing if you forsake yourself

It was the only right thing to do,
be calm, your home is here

Then I looked out of my chair through the open window
I really don't have much desire to do that
The only thing I do desire
I won't do that either

Monday

You can achieve m

It was the only nigh
be calm, you know

Then I looked out at m
I really don't have
The only thing I do des
I won't do that eit

t you torsela yourself

to do,

i Through the open window
desire to do That

Fence Books is an extension of **FENCE**, a biannual journal of poetry, fiction, art, and criticism that has a mission to redefine the terms of accessibility by publishing challenging writing distinguished by idiosyncrasy and intelligence rather than by allegiance with camps, schools, or cliques. It is part of our press's mission to support writers who might otherwise have difficulty being recognized because their work doesn't answer to either the mainstream or to recognizable modes of experimentation.

The Alberta Prize is an annual series administered by Fence Books in collaboration with the Alberta duPont Bonsal Foundation. The Alberta Prize offers publication of a first or second book of poems by a woman, as well as a five thousand dollar cash prize.

Our second prize series is the **Fence Modern Poets Series.** This contest is open to poets of either gender and at any stage of career, and offers a one thousand dollar cash prize in addition to book publication.

For more information about either prize, visit **www.fencebooks.com**, or send an SASE to: Fence Books/[Name of Prize], 303 East Eighth Street, #B1, New York, New York, 10009.

For more about **FENCE**, visit **www.fencemag.com**.

FENCE BOOKS

The Alberta Prize

Practice, Restraint	Laura Sims
A Magic Book	Sasha Steensen
Sky Girl	Rosemary Griggs
The Real Moon of Poetry and Other Poems	Tina Celona
Zirconia	Chelsey Minnis

Fence Modern Poets Series

The Stupefying Flashbulbs	Daniel Brenner, judge Rebecca Wolff
Povel	Geraldine Kim, judge Forrest Gander
The Opening Question	Prageeta Sharma, judge Peter Gizzi
Apprehend	Elizabeth Robinson, judge Ann Lauterbach
The Red Bird	Joyelle McSweeney, judge Allen Grossman

Free Choice

Swallows	Martin Corless-Smith
Folding Ruler Star	Aaron Kunin
The Commandrine and Other Poems	Joyelle McSweeney
Macular Hole	Catherine Wagner
Nota	Martin Corless-Smith
Father of Noise	Anthony McCann
Can You Relax in My House	Michael Earl Craig
s America	Catherine Wagner